SEP 2013

W9-CJQ-375

EDGE BOOKS™

SUPER TRIVIA COLLECTION

THIS
BOOK
MIGHT BLOW
YOU AWAY

BY KAREN M. LEET

A COLLECTION OF
AMAZING WEATHER
TRIVIA

Content Consultant:
Joseph Moran, PhD
Meteorologist, Education Program
American Meteorological Society

CAPSTONE PRESS
a capstone imprint

Edge Books are published by Capstone Press,
1710 Roe Crest Drive, North Mankato, Minnesota 56003.
www.capstonepub.com

Library of Congress Cataloging-in-Publication Data
Leet, Karen M.
This book might blow you away : a collection of amazing weather trivia / by Karen Leet.
    p. cm. — (Edge books. Super trivia collection)
Audience: 8-13
Audience: 4 to 6
Summary: "Describes a variety of trivia facts about weather"— Provided by publisher.
Includes bibliographical references and index.
ISBN 978-1-4296-8421-7 (library binding)
ISBN 978-1-62065-234-3 (ebook PDF)
1. Weather—Miscellanea—Juvenile literature. I. Title.
QC981.3.L44 2013
551.6—dc23   2012004672

Editorial Credits
Angie Kaelberer, editor; Tracy McCabe, designer; Wanda Winch, media specialist;
    Laura Manthe, production specialist

Photo Credits
Alex Tomlinson, 8 (bottom); AP Images, 6 (top), 17 (t); Corbis: Ultimate Chase/Mike Theiss,
17 (b); Dr. A. Santhosh Kumar, 15 (b); Dreamstime: Cholder, 26 (t), Darko Plohl, 9 (t), Darren
Bradley, 25 (m), Dmitri Melnik, 27 (t), Michael R. Brown, 7 (t), Miknik, 10 (t), Rob Stegmann,
19 (t), Scottmiller2, 13 (t); Getty Images: David McNew, 18 (b); iStockphoto: Rob Broek, 18
(t), Johnstown Area Heritage Association (JAHA), 14 (b); Library of Congress: Prints and
Photographs Division, 20, 29 (t); Minden Pictures: Jim Brandenburg, 15 (t); NASA: Astronaut
Mike Fincke, 22 (t); Newscom: Lonely Planet Images/Ralph Hopkins, 14 (t), Miami Herald
Pool/Peter Andrew Bosch, 22 (b), PacificCoastNews/Kevin Perkins, 28 (t), Splash/Sebastian
Allan, 8 (t), Zuma Press, 10 (b); NOAA: Les Scott, 12; Shutterstock: Aivolie, 25 (b), AKV, 5
(bees), 26 (b), Albachiaraa, 25 (t), B747, cover (mb), Christos Georghiou, cover (bl), Daniel
Loretto, 29 (b), Dietmar Hoepfl, 9 (m), Eclipse Digital, 11 (Texas outline), Etienne du Preez,
cover (tl), Fernando Cortes, graffiti design, George Nazmi Bebawi, cover (tr), happy dancing,
5 (t), Joellen L Armstrong, 10 (m), JustASC, 21, Klara Viskova, 27 (m), lafoto, 9 (b), lavitrei,
13 (b), Leonidtit, 5 (mr), Melanie Metz, 16, Pushkin, 4, Sashkin, 11 (b), Sebastian Tomus, 17
(m), Sergej Khakimullin, 5 (b), sima, 11 (t), Studio Barcelona, 6 (b), TyBy, 11 (lighting bolt),
Vladislav Gurfinkel, cover (br), Zastol'skiy Victor Leonidovich, 28 (b); STScI: NASA/R. Beebe,
A. Simon (NMSU), 23; Tim Tevebaugh, 24; University of Chicago, 19 (b); Weldon Owen
Publishing: Dr. Mark A. Garlick, artist, 27 (b); Wikipedia: Russell and Sydney Poore, 7 (b)

Printed in the United States of America in Stevens Point, Wisconsin.

032012   006678WZF12

TABLE OF CONTENTS

Introduction: ALL KINDS OF WEATHER 4

Chapter 1: ZAP AND BOOM 6

Chapter 2: WHAT'S FALLING FROM THE SKY? 12

Chapter 3: STORMS CALLED TWISTERS 16

Chapter 4: HAZARDOUS HURRICANES 20

Chapter 5: WEATHER WEIRDNESS 24

Glossary...30

Read More......................................31

Internet Sites.................................31

Index..32

Introduction
ALL KINDS OF WEATHER

Have you ever seen watermelon snow or hissing, exploding ball lighting? Or a snowflake the size of a pizza? And did you know bees and sharks predict weather?

Weather is something we experience every day. But it's much more than wind, rain, snow, and sunshine. The world of weather is full of facts that are almost too amazing to be true. Have fun discovering the world's weirdest, wildest weather trivia!

Chapter 1

ZAP AND BOOM

Flash! Bolts of lightning slash across the sky. Rain drums on the roof. Thunder roars and booms. Wind rattles windows, and tree branches crash to the ground. Powerful thunderstorms can cause plenty of damage and strange events.

What was so odd about Shenandoah National Park Ranger Roy Sullivan? He was nicknamed the Human Lightning Rod. Between 1942 and 1977, he was zapped seven times—most likely by a bolt that hit something he was touching. Two of those times, his hair caught fire!

Just how hot is lightning? Lightning can heat the air in its path to 50,000 degrees Fahrenheit (27,760 degrees Celsius). That's five times hotter than the sun's surface!

Central Florida is known as the lightning capital of the United States. During an average August in Brevard County, Florida, lightning strikes more than 6,000 times!

A statue in Lexington, Kentucky, has the worst luck around. A powerful thunderstorm in July 1903 hit a statue of politician Henry Clay that stood atop a 120-foot (37-meter) stone column. The storm knocked off the statue's 350-pound (159-kilogram) head. The headless statue was fixed in May 1910. Four months later, lightning shattered the statue again. Now it has a **lightning rod** for protection.

lightning rod—a metal rod that carries a lightning charge safely into the ground

Lightning is attracted to tall buildings. Lightning strikes the 1,454-foot (443-m) Empire State Building in New York City about 100 times each year.

Mysterious ball lightning slips inside houses through windows, doors, or chimneys. As large as a soccer ball or as tiny as a grape, some ball lightning glows bright white. Or it can be red, orange, yellow, green, blue, or violet.
It bounces, floats, buzzes, and hisses. Then it disappears or explodes. Scientists still aren't sure what causes it.

Cows and lightning don't mix. To escape from a storm, cows often huddle under trees. If lightning hits the trees, it can kill the whole herd—31 in a single strike in Denmark in 2004. Or cows rush to a wire fence. Lightning zaps the fence and kills the cows—52 dead cows in Uruguay in October 2008.

It's a good rule to stay away from trees, metal fences, and cows during a thunderstorm!

No storm in sight. Bright, blue sky. Think lightning won't hit? Wrong! Lightning can strike 10 to 15 miles (16 to 24 kilometers) away from a storm. These strikes are called bolts from the blue.

Hundreds of years ago, people in Europe thought noise scared away lightning storms. Men rushed to the top of towers to ring church bells. Not a good idea—nearly 400 bell towers were struck and more than 100 bell ringers died.

In summer the sky sometimes flashes with "heat lightning." But there's no boom or rumble of thunder. That's because light travels much faster than sound. You can see the lightning from a distant storm, but it's too far away to hear the thunder.

A woman struck and killed by lightning in Pennsylvania in 1994 was found with the zipper of her jeans melted. Plus, two coins in her pocket were fused together.

What could lightning and ribbons have in common? Ribbon lightning occurs when strong winds separate the strokes of the bolt, making it look like a wide ribbon.

At 120 **decibels**, thunder is almost as noisy as a jackhammer. Get too close, and you could have temporary deafness or even permanent hearing loss.

An average lightning bolt is 5 miles (8 km) long. The longest ever recorded spanned 118 miles (190 km) near Dallas, Texas!

During a thunderstorm, you can figure out the distance of lightning. When you see lightning, count the seconds until you hear thunder. Divide the number by five. The result is the number of miles between you and the lightning.

decibel—a unit for measuring the volume of sound

Chapter 2

WHAT'S FALLING FROM THE SKY?

You never know what might fall from the sky. A heavy downpour could flatten your mom's flowers. Hail might pound dents in your family car. Snow may pile so high that schools and businesses close. Even frogs can fall from the sky!

Volleyball-sized hailstones pelted Vivian, South Dakota, on July 23, 2010. Imagine a 2-pound (0.9-kg) hailstone hitting your car or your house's roof. Clunk!

A deadly hailstorm in India on April 30, 1988, killed 246 people and about 1,600 animals. With no warning, the daytime sky turned black, and hailstones the size of baseballs pounded people before they could find shelter.

Snowflakes the size of large pizzas fell from the sky on January 28, 1887, at Fort Keough, Montana. The flakes were said to be 15 inches (38 cm) wide and 8 inches (20 cm) thick. When snow crystals clump together, gigantic snowflakes can form.

The bigger a hailstone, the faster it falls to the ground. Large hailstones can fall faster than 100 miles (161 km) per hour!

Keep your umbrella handy! Reports during the past hundreds of years describe frogs, fish, and even maggots tumbling from the sky. Researchers suspect tornadic **waterspouts** suck up the creatures and later drop them again.

waterspout—a mass of spinning wind that stretches from a cloud to a body of water

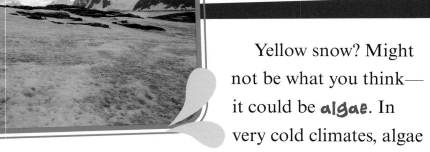

Yellow snow? Might not be what you think— it could be **algae**. In very cold climates, algae can grow in snow, turning it yellow, blue, or brown. "Watermelon snow" in polar regions can be red or green and smells sweet, like a melon. Dust, sand, and pollen can also cause colored snow. You probably still shouldn't eat it.

The rain just wouldn't stop in Johnstown, Pennsylvania, late in May 1889. On May 31 the South Fork Dam on Lake Conemaugh gave way. Twenty million tons (18 million metric tons) of lake water roared down the valley. The **flash flood** and the fire that followed it killed 2,209 people, making it one of the worst disasters in U.S. history.

algae—plants without roots or stems that grow in water

flash flood—a flood that occurs with little or no warning

No one can control the weather, but people have tried. "Cloud seeding" began in the 1940s. Airplane pilots dropped dry ice pellets or **silver iodide** into clouds. These substances caused the clouds to develop snow, which melted into raindrops as it fell. People in some drought-stricken areas still use cloud seeding.

Lightning flashes and booming thunder during a snowstorm? It happens! Thundersnow can occur when a layer of moist, warm air near the ground pushes upward through a layer of cold air.

In Kerala, India, blood-red rain fell from the sky occasionally from late July to September 2001. Was it caused by red dust? Fungus spores? Or **microbes** from outer space? Nobody knows for sure.

silver iodide—a chemical used in cloud seeding

microbe—a living thing that is too small to be seen without a microscope

STORMS CALLED TWISTERS

Also called twisters, tornadoes can be huge, incredibly powerful, and unpredictable. A tornado can demolish a house in a heartbeat or hop over and never touch it. A tornado can be skinny and funnel-shaped or so wide it's like a thick, dark wall of wind.

Keep your eyes on the sky if you live in Tornado Alley! In the center of the United States, tornadoes hit more often and are more severe. This is especially the case in Nebraska, Kansas, Oklahoma and Texas. But twisters can also strike almost anyplace else.

On April 3 and 4, 1974, a "Super Outbreak" caused 148 tornadoes in 13 states. In Xenia, Ohio, a school bus landed on a stage where high school students had been rehearsing a play! The students escaped just minutes before the tornado struck.

People in Codell, Kansas, might be a little nervous every May 20. On May 20, 1916, a tornado roared through town. On May 20, 1917, another tornado struck the town. A year later another tornado hit Codell on—you guessed it—May 20.

Tornado winds can do some very strange things. They can whisk away egg cartons without breaking eggs. Twisters can blow papers hundreds of miles away or jam a splinter into a metal fire hydrant. A tornado in Great Bend, Kansas, carried a tie rack 40 miles (64 km) away without losing the ties.

Ever seen spouts of water or dirt spinning in the air? Waterspouts can suck up fish and sink ships. Dust devils can be tiny whirlwinds of dirt or towers of spinning sand. Dust devils often last only a minute, but some contain tons of dust whirling thousands of feet high.

About 1,000 tornadoes rage through the United States each year, striking any month, any time, day or night. April 2011 had a record-breaking 758 tornadoes!

Can a tornado catch fire? No, but wildfires sometimes form a rotating column that looks much like a tornado. Fire whirls are usually caused by a great deal of heat produced in a small space. After the Great Kanto earthquake in Japan in 1923, a fire whirl killed 38,000 people trapped in downtown Tokyo.

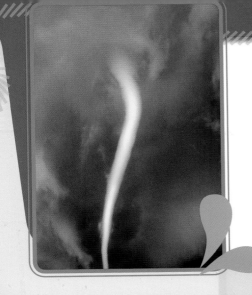

What color is a tornado? A tornado that forms in **humid** air may have a cloud inside it, making it appear white. Tornadoes can also be black, brown, red or gray, depending on the color of dirt and **debris** they pick up.

Enhanced Fujita Scale

In 1971 Dr. Tetsuya Theodore Fujita developed a scale for measuring tornado severity by wind speed. Fujita's scale was updated in 2007, becoming the Enhanced Fujita (EF) scale used today.

EF Number	3-second gust (mph)
0	65–85
1	86–110
2	111–135
3	136–165
4	166–200
5	more than 200

humid—damp and moist

debris—the scattered pieces of something that has been broken or destroyed

Chapter 4

HAZARDOUS HURRICANES

Hurricanes are big, bold, and bad. These gigantic storms form in warm tropical ocean waters and gather strength as they barrel toward land. Hurricanes can be amazingly hard to predict. They can speed up or slow down as they approach, sometimes stalling for days. They can pound coastal cities with destructive winds, drenching rain, and a wall of seawater.

Before hurricanes had names, a massive hurricane smashed into Galveston Island, Texas, in 1900. A **storm surge** of 8 to 15 feet (2.4 to 4.6 m) covered the island. It was the worst weather disaster in U.S. history, killing at least 8,000 people.

storm surge—a dome of ocean water that sweeps over a coastal area

In 1953 the U.S. Weather Bureau started naming hurricanes and tropical storms using an alphabetical list. At first storms had only women's names. In 1979 men's names were added. Could you share a name with a hurricane? Check the National Weather Service's web site for the hurricane name list. If your name starts with Q, U, X, Y or Z, don't bother looking. Hurricane names don't begin with those letters.

Some hurricanes are so destructive their names are retired and never used again. Terrible storms like Hazel in 1954, Camille in 1969, and Andrew in 1992 got those names retired.

Retired Hurricane Names

Between 2000 and 2010, 26 hurricane names have been retired.

2000—Keith
2001—Allison, Iris, Michelle
2002—Isidore, Lili
2003—Fabian, Isabel, Juan
2004—Charley, Frances, Ivan, Jeanne
2005—Dennis, Katrina, Rita, Stan, Wilma

2006—none retired
2007—Dean, Felix, Noel
2008—Gustav, Ike, Paloma
2009—none retired
2010—Igor, Tomas

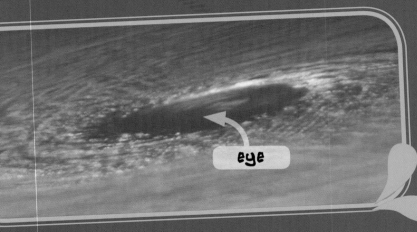

eye

At the center of even the wildest hurricane is a calm, quiet "eye" that can fool people into thinking the storm is over. But after the eye passes, pounding rain and howling winds slam back as fierce as ever.

Tornadoes and hurricanes often go hand-in-hand. In 2004 Hurricane Ivan caused a whopping 117 tornadoes in three days!

Hurricanes generally last only a few days once they hit land. But a storm very similar to a hurricane has been raging on Jupiter for at least 300 years!

On July 27, 1943, over the Gulf of Mexico, U.S. Colonel Joseph Duckworth twice flew his single-engine plane into the eye of a hurricane. He landed safely both times. Duckworth was the very first "hurricane hunter"—and he did it on a dare! Hurricane hunters have been monitoring hurricane conditions by plane ever since.

Saffir-Simpson Hurricane Scale

Herb Saffir and Bob Simpson developed the Saffir-Simpson scale in 1971. The scale uses wind speed to measure hurricane severity.

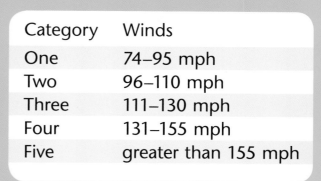

Category	Winds
One	74–95 mph
Two	96–110 mph
Three	111–130 mph
Four	131–155 mph
Five	greater than 155 mph

Chapter 5

WEATHER WEIRDNESS

Scientists who study weather track storms and predict what they might do next. Scientists can give warnings and safety advice. They can save lives with advances in weather technology. But nobody can be totally certain what weather will do next—and nobody can control it. Weather can be amazing, awesome, and absolutely bizarre.

Nature can shape snowballs without any human help. Wind can roll snow into large **cylinders** 2 feet (0.6 m) wide. To form, these snow rollers need gusty winds and temperatures just above freezing. A layer of ice needs to be on the ground, covered with a layer of new, fluffy snow.

cylinder—a tube-shaped solid with circular ends

The coldest recorded temperature in North America was on February 3, 1947. At Snag Airport in the Canadian Yukon, the temperature hit minus 81°F (-63°C). Spit froze before reaching the ground. Breath hung in the air like fog. Eyes watered and nose hairs froze. Brr!

In Baker, California, the world's largest thermometer towers 134 feet (41 m) high. Its height matches the hottest North American temperature, 134°F (57°C), which was set in 1913 in Death Valley, California.

Niagara Falls, the most powerful waterfall in North America, stopped on March 29, 1848. For hours, not a drop of water trickled over the falls because of an ice jam on the upper Niagara River.

In Phoenix, Arizona, the summer of 2011 was a bad season for dust! Monster dust storms struck three times, knocking out power, halting airline flights, and coating everything with dirt. Called haboobs, these gigantic walls of sand can be 50 miles (80 km) wide and more than 1 mile (1.61 km) high!

One way to predict the weather is to watch wild animals. Before a thunderstorm, birds head for their nests and bees zoom for their hives. Before a hurricane, sharks swim for safety in deeper water.

Pinecones are a good indicator of weather. On dry days pinecones open up wide to disperse seeds. On damp days pinecones close up tight.

Do you love lying out in the sun? Yuma, Arizona, is the place for you. It's nearly always sunny in Yuma—at least 90 percent of the time. It's the sunniest spot in the world!

Snow in June in New England. Lakes frozen in July and August in Pennsylvania. Widespread crop failures. It was 1816, the "year without a summer." All because a series of volcanic eruptions, ending with Mount Tambora in Indonesia, shot ash and dust into the sky. That volcanic debris brought global cooling and a snowy summer.

Hurricanes and tornadoes are known for their fierce winds. But strong winds don't always come with a storm. In December 2011 powerful winds blew through Southern California at gusts of 97 miles (156 km) per hour—equal to a Category 2 hurricane!

A massive **drought** hit the United States in the 1930s. Without rain, crops died. Without crops to hold the soil in place, soil turned dry and dusty. Wind lifted that dust into huge, billowing storms.

In 1932, 14 dust storms swept through the central states. By 1933, 38 huge dust storms struck. Farmland blew away—100 million acres (40 million hectares) of it!

drought—a long time with little or no rainfall

April 14, 1935, called Black Sunday, brought the worst dust storms. Powerful "black blizzards" even reached New York and Washington, D.C.!

Now that you know about the world's weirdest weather, be prepared and aware. Learn what to do when wild weather strikes. Find the facts on weather safety, so you know what to do in case of tornadoes, floods, lightning, blizzards, and more. Be an expert who can outsmart the wildest weather whenever it shows up.

GLOSSARY

algae (AL-jee)—plants without roots or stems that grow in water

cylinder (SI-luhn-duhr)—a tube-shaped object with circular ends

debris (duh-BREE)—the scattered pieces of something that has been broken or destroyed

decibel (DE-suh-buhl)—a unit for measuring the volume of sounds

drought (DROUT)—a long period of weather with little or no rainfall

flash flood (FLASH FLUHD)—a flood that occurs with little or no warning

humid (HYOO-mid)—damp and moist

lightning rod (LITE-ning ROD)—a metal rod that carries a lightning charge safely into the ground

microbe (MYE-krobe)— a living thing that is too small to see without a microscope

silver iodide (SIL-vur EYE-uh-dyed)—a chemical used in cloud seeding

storm surge (STORM SURJ)—a dome of ocean water 50 to 100 miles (80 to 160 km) wide that sweeps over a coastal area, causing flooding

waterspout (WAW-tur-spowt)—a mass of spinning wind that stretches from a cloud to a body of water

READ MORE

Birch, Robin. *Extreme Weather*. Weather and Climate. New York: Marshall Cavendish Benchmark, 2009.

Furgang, Kathy. *Weather: Facts, Photos, and Fun that Will Blow You Away*. National Geographic Kids Everything. Washington, D.C.: National Geographic, 2012.

Gifford, Clive. *Chasing the World's Most Dangerous Storms*. Extreme Explorations. Mankato, Minn.: Capstone Press, 2010.

Levete, Sarah. *Catastrophic Weather*. Protecting Our Planet. New York: Crabtree, 2010.

INTERNET SITES

FactHound offers a safe, fun way to find Internet sites related to this book. All of the sites on FactHound have been researched by our staff.

Here's all you do:

Visit *www.facthound.com*

Type in this code: 9781429684217

Super-cool stuff! Check out projects, games and lots more at
www.capstonekids.com

INDEX

animal predictions, 4, 26

cloud seeding, 15

drought, 15, 28
Duckworth, Joseph, 23
dust devils, 18
dust storms, 26, 28, 29
    Black Sunday, 29
    haboobs, 26

Empire State Building, 8
Enhanced Fujita (EF) scale, 19

floods, 14, 29

hail, 12, 13
hurricanes, 20–23, 26, 28
    eyes, 22, 23
    names, 20, 21
    storm surges, 20

Jupiter, 23

lightning, 6–11, 15, 29
    ball lightning, 8
    bolts from the blue, 9
    heat lightning, 10
    ribbon lightning, 10

Mount Tambora, 27

National Weather Service, 21
Niagara Falls, 25

pinecones, 27

rain, 4, 6, 14, 15, 20, 22, 28
    red rain, 15

Saffir-Simpson hurricane
    scale, 23
snow, 4, 12, 13, 14, 15, 24, 27, 29
    snow cylinders, 24
    watermelon snow, 14
Sullivan, Roy, 6
sunshine, 4, 27

temperatures, 6, 24, 25
thundersnow, 15
thunderstorms, 6, 7, 9, 10, 11, 26
tornadoes, 16–19, 22, 28, 29
    fire whirls, 18
    Super Outbreak, 17
    Tornado Alley, 16

waterspouts, 13, 18

"year without a summer," 27